EMMANUEL JOSEPH

Mindscapes and Landscapes, Exploring the Psychological Roots of Environmental Art

Contents

1

Chapter 1: The Essence of Environmental Art

Art is a reflection of the world around us, capturing the essence of nature and the environment in which we live. Environmental art goes beyond mere representation, delving into the emotional and psychological connections we have with our surroundings. It challenges us to see the world through different lenses, exploring the deep-rooted relationship between humans and nature. From ancient cave paintings to contemporary installations, environmental art has always been a medium to express our innermost thoughts and feelings about the world we inhabit. Through this art form, we can better understand our own psychological landscape and how it shapes our perception of the natural world.

Environmental art often involves direct interaction with the environment, using natural materials and landscapes as the canvas. This art form is not confined to galleries or museums but can be found in forests, deserts, oceans, and urban spaces. One example is the work of Andy Goldsworthy, a British sculptor and environmental artist known for his site-specific installations made from natural materials like leaves, stones, and ice. Goldsworthy's art is ephemeral, highlighting the transient nature of the environment and our fleeting connection to it.

The essence of environmental art lies in its ability to evoke a sense of wonder and contemplation. It invites viewers to reflect on their relationship with the environment and consider the impact of their actions on the natural world. By engaging with environmental art, we can develop a deeper appreciation for the beauty and fragility of the ecosystems that sustain us. It serves as a reminder that we are not separate from nature but are intrinsically connected to it.

Moreover, environmental art can inspire change by raising awareness about pressing environmental issues. Artists use their work to highlight the consequences of pollution, deforestation, climate change, and other threats to the environment. Through powerful visual narratives, they can convey the urgency of protecting our planet for future generations. For instance, the artist Agnes Denes created "Wheatfield – A Confrontation," where she planted a two-acre wheat field in downtown Manhattan in 1982. The project drew attention to the stark contrast between urban development and agricultural land, sparking conversations about sustainability and food security.

In conclusion, environmental art is a profound and transformative art form that captures the essence of our connection with nature. It challenges us to see the world differently, fostering a deeper understanding of our psychological landscape and its influence on our perception of the environment. Through the works of artists like Andy Goldsworthy and Agnes Denes, we can appreciate the beauty and complexity of the natural world and be inspired to take action to protect it.

2

Chapter 2: The Birth of Environmental Art

The origins of environmental art can be traced back to prehistoric times when early humans created cave paintings and carvings that depicted their interactions with nature. These early artworks were not just representations of the world around them but also held deep symbolic meanings. As civilizations evolved, so did the art forms, with different cultures developing their unique ways of expressing their connection to the environment. The Renaissance period marked a significant shift in the depiction of nature, with artists like Leonardo da Vinci and Michelangelo incorporating elements of the natural world into their masterpieces. This chapter explores the evolution of environmental art and how it has shaped our understanding of the world.

In the earliest days, prehistoric humans expressed their relationship with nature through cave paintings, such as those found in Lascaux, France, and Altamira, Spain. These artworks often depicted animals, hunting scenes, and natural landscapes, serving as both a record of daily life and a means of spiritual connection with the environment. The use of natural pigments and materials in these paintings reflects the close bond early humans had with their surroundings.

As human societies developed, so too did their artistic expressions. Ancient civilizations like the Egyptians, Greeks, and Romans created elaborate artworks that incorporated natural elements. The Egyptians, for example, used symbols of the natural world, such as the lotus flower and the scarab beetle, to convey their beliefs about life, death, and rebirth. Greek and Roman artists, on the other hand, celebrated the beauty of the natural world through detailed sculptures and frescoes depicting gods, goddesses, and mythological creatures intertwined with nature.

The Renaissance period marked a significant turning point in the depiction of nature in art. Artists like Leonardo da Vinci and Michelangelo sought to capture the beauty and complexity of the natural world in their works. Da Vinci's detailed studies of plants, animals, and landscapes, as seen in his famous notebooks, reflect his deep curiosity about the natural world and its underlying principles. Michelangelo's frescoes in the Sistine Chapel, with their intricate depictions of the natural world, demonstrate his mastery of form and composition, drawing inspiration from the environment around him.

The Romantic movement of the 18th and 19th centuries further emphasized the emotional and psychological connections between humans and nature. Artists like Caspar David Friedrich and J.M.W. Turner used their works to explore the sublime beauty and power of the natural world, often depicting dramatic landscapes and seascapes that evoked a sense of awe and wonder. Their paintings served as a reminder of the inherent connection between humans and nature, encouraging viewers to reflect on their place within the larger ecological system.

In the 20th century, environmental art evolved to address contemporary concerns about the environment. Artists like Robert Smithson and Nancy Holt created large-scale land art installations that integrated natural landscapes with artistic interventions. Smithson's "Spiral Jetty," a massive earthwork constructed in the Great Salt Lake, and Holt's "Sun Tunnels," a series of concrete tunnels aligned with the sun's solstices, exemplify the ways in which environmental art can merge with the natural world to create thought-provoking and immersive experiences.

In conclusion, the birth and evolution of environmental art have been deeply intertwined with humanity's relationship with nature. From prehistoric cave paintings to contemporary land art installations, environmental art has continually evolved to reflect our changing understanding of the natural world. By exploring the rich history of environmental art, we can gain a deeper appreciation for the diverse ways in which artists have expressed their connection to the environment throughout the ages.

3

Chapter 3: The Role of Psychology in Art

Psychology plays a crucial role in the creation and interpretation of art. Environmental art, in particular, taps into our subconscious mind, evoking emotions and memories that are deeply rooted in our psyche. Artists often draw inspiration from their personal experiences and emotions, creating works that resonate with the viewer on a psychological level. Understanding the psychological aspects of environmental art can help us appreciate the deeper meanings behind the artworks and how they influence our perception of the world. This chapter delves into the psychological theories that underpin environmental art and how they shape our understanding of this unique art form.

The relationship between art and psychology can be traced back to the early 20th century with the advent of psychoanalysis. Sigmund Freud's theories on the unconscious mind and the role of dreams and memories in shaping behavior had a profound impact on artists of the time. Surrealists like Salvador Dalí and René Magritte used their art to explore the hidden depths of the human psyche, creating dream-like landscapes that challenged conventional notions of reality. Environmental artists, too, have drawn on these psychological concepts to create works that evoke a sense of mystery and introspection.

Carl Jung, another influential psychologist, introduced the concept of the collective unconscious, a shared reservoir of memories and archetypes that influence human behavior. Jung's ideas have been instrumental in shaping our understanding of environmental art. Artists often tap into these universal symbols and motifs, creating works that resonate with viewers on a deep, instinctual level. For example, the use of natural elements like water, trees, and animals in environmental art can evoke a sense of familiarity and connection, reminding us of our shared heritage and the primal bond we have with nature.

Environmental art also draws on the principles of gestalt psychology, which emphasizes the human tendency to perceive patterns and wholes rather than isolated elements. Artists use this concept to create immersive and cohesive experiences that engage the viewer's mind and senses. By carefully arranging natural materials and landscapes, environmental artists can guide the viewer's perception and create a sense of harmony and balance. This approach not only enhances the aesthetic appeal of the artwork but also reinforces the message of interconnectedness between humans and the environment.

The psychological impact of environmental art extends beyond the individual viewer to the collective consciousness of society. Art has the power to shape cultural narratives and influence public opinion. Environmental artists use their work to challenge prevailing attitudes and beliefs about the natural world, encouraging viewers to question their relationship with the environment and consider alternative perspectives. This process of cognitive reframing can lead to a shift in perception and behavior, fostering a greater sense of environmental responsibility and stewardship.

In conclusion, the role of psychology in environmental art is multifaceted and profound. By tapping into the subconscious mind and drawing on psychological theories, artists can create works that resonate deeply with viewers and evoke powerful emotions and memories. Understanding the psychological underpinnings of environmental art can help us appreciate the deeper meanings and messages behind the artworks, enriching our experience and connection with the natural world.

4

Chapter 4: The Power of Nature in Art

Nature has always been a powerful source of inspiration for artists. The beauty and majesty of the natural world have the ability to evoke a wide range of emotions, from awe and wonder to fear and despair. Environmental artists use their work to capture the essence of nature and convey its impact on the human psyche. Through their art, they can highlight the fragility of the environment and the urgent need to protect it. This chapter explores the different ways in which nature influences environmental art and how artists use their work to raise awareness about environmental issues.

One of the most compelling aspects of environmental art is its ability to evoke a sense of wonder and reverence for the natural world. Artists like Ansel Adams and Georgia O'Keeffe have captured the breathtaking beauty of landscapes through their photography and paintings, respectively. Adams' black-and-white photographs of Yosemite National Park and O'Keeffe's vibrant depictions of the American Southwest both convey a deep appreciation for the natural world and its inherent grandeur.

Environmental art can also serve as a powerful commentary on the impact of human activities on the environment. Artists like Chris Jordan and Olafur Eliasson create works that highlight the consequences of pollution, climate change, and habitat destruction. Jordan's "Running the Numbers" series, for example, uses large-scale photographs to illustrate the staggering scale of consumer waste and its environmental impact. Eliasson's "Ice Watch" installation, which involved placing large blocks of melting ice in urban spaces, served as a poignant reminder of the effects of climate change on polar ice caps.

The use of natural materials and processes in environmental art can further enhance the connection between the artwork and the environment. Artists like Nils-Udo and Richard Long create site-specific installations using natural elements such as stones, leaves, and branches. These works are often temporary and subject to the forces of nature, emphasizing the transient and ever-changing nature of the environment. By incorporating natural materials into their art, these artists create a direct link between the artwork and the landscape, inviting viewers to reflect on their own relationship with the natural world.

In addition to raising awareness about environmental issues, environmental art can also inspire a sense of hope and possibility. Artists like Maya Lin and Patrick Dougherty create works that celebrate the resilience and beauty of nature, offering a vision of a more sustainable and harmonious future. Lin's "Wavefield" series, for example, features undulating earthworks that mimic the patterns of ocean waves, symbolizing the interconnectedness of land and sea. Dougherty's whimsical "stickwork" sculptures, made from woven branches, evoke a sense of playfulness and wonder, reminding us of the joy and creativity that can be found in nature.

In conclusion, the power of nature in environmental art lies in its ability to evoke a wide range of emotions and provoke thoughtful reflection. By capturing the beauty and majesty of the natural world, highlighting the impact of human activities, and using natural materials and processes, environmental artists create works that resonate deeply with viewers and inspire a greater appreciation for the environment. Through their art, they can raise awareness about pressing environmental issues and foster a sense of hope and possibility for a more sustainable future.

5

Chapter 5: The Influence of Culture on Environmental Art

Culture plays a significant role in shaping our perception of the environment and, consequently, environmental art. Different cultures have their unique ways of interpreting and representing the natural world, influenced by their beliefs, traditions, and values. For instance, Indigenous art often reflects a deep spiritual connection with the land, while Western art may focus more on the aesthetic beauty of nature. This chapter examines the cultural influences on environmental art and how they contribute to the diversity of this art form. Through a comparative analysis, we can gain a deeper understanding of how different cultures perceive and interact with the environment.

Indigenous cultures around the world have a profound connection with the land, viewing it as a living entity with its own spirit and consciousness. This deep bond is often reflected in their art, which serves as a means of communication with the natural world. For example, Australian Aboriginal art is rich with symbols and patterns that represent the Dreamtime stories of creation, connecting the people with their ancestral lands. Similarly, Native American art often features motifs of animals, plants, and landscapes, symbolizing the interconnectedness of all living beings.

In contrast, Western art has historically emphasized the aesthetic and recreational aspects of nature. During the Romantic period, artists like J.M.W. Turner and Caspar David Friedrich depicted dramatic landscapes that evoked a sense of awe and the sublime. Their works celebrated the beauty and power of nature, reflecting a more human-centered perspective. However, contemporary Western environmental artists are increasingly addressing ecological concerns, using their art to advocate for environmental protection and sustainability.

Cultural influences on environmental art are also evident in the use of materials and techniques. For example, Japanese art often incorporates elements of nature, such as bamboo and cherry blossoms, using traditional techniques like ink painting and woodblock printing. The Japanese concept of "wabi-sabi," which appreciates the beauty of imperfection and impermanence, is reflected in environmental art that embraces the transient nature of the environment.

The cultural diversity in environmental art enriches our understanding of the natural world and our place within it. By exploring the unique perspectives and expressions of different cultures, we can gain a deeper appreciation for the interconnectedness of all life and the importance of protecting our shared environment. This chapter highlights the importance of cultural diversity in environmental art and how it can inspire a more inclusive and holistic approach to environmental stewardship.

6

Chapter 6: The Intersection of Science and Art

Science and art may seem like two opposing fields, but they often intersect in the realm of environmental art. Scientific discoveries and advancements have provided artists with new tools and techniques to create their work. Conversely, environmental art can help communicate complex scientific concepts in a more accessible and engaging way. This chapter explores the relationship between science and art, highlighting how environmental artists use scientific knowledge to inform their work. Through this intersection, we can gain a deeper appreciation of the natural world and the intricate balance that sustains it.

Environmental artists often draw on scientific principles to create works that explore the natural world and its processes. For example, the artist Mark Dion uses scientific methods of collecting and categorizing to create installations that resemble natural history exhibits. His work challenges the traditional boundaries between science and art, encouraging viewers to question their perceptions of the natural world. Similarly, the artist Agnes Denes created "Tree Mountain – A Living Time Capsule," a large-scale land art project in Finland that involved planting 11,000 trees in a precise geometric pattern. The project combines ecological restoration with artistic expression, highlighting the interconnectedness of art and science.

The use of technology in environmental art also demonstrates the intersection of science and art. Digital tools and techniques, such as computer modeling and virtual reality, allow artists to create immersive experiences that engage the viewer's senses and imagination. For example, the artist Olafur Eliasson uses technology to create interactive installations that explore natural phenomena like light, water, and weather. His work, "The Weather Project," installed in the Turbine Hall of the Tate Modern, used mist, mirrors, and artificial sunlight to create an atmospheric environment that captivated visitors and encouraged them to reflect on their relationship with the natural world.

Environmental art can also serve as a powerful tool for communicating scientific concepts and raising awareness about environmental issues. Artists like Maya Lin use their work to visualize data and make complex information more accessible to the public. Lin's project, "What is Missing?" is a multimedia installation that uses sound, video, and interactive elements to highlight the global biodiversity crisis. By presenting scientific data in an engaging and creative way, environmental artists can inspire action and promote environmental stewardship.

In conclusion, the intersection of science and art in environmental art offers a unique and powerful way to explore and understand the natural world. By drawing on scientific principles and using technology, artists can create works that engage the viewer's senses and imagination, making complex concepts more accessible and inspiring a greater appreciation for the environment. This chapter highlights the importance of integrating science and art to foster a deeper understanding of the natural world and promote environmental awareness.

7

Chapter 7: The Role of Technology in Environmental Art

Technology has revolutionized the way we create and experience art. Environmental artists are now able to use digital tools and techniques to bring their visions to life in ways that were previously unimaginable. From virtual reality installations to interactive digital artworks, technology has opened up new possibilities for environmental art. This chapter examines the impact of technology on environmental art and how it has transformed the way we perceive and interact with the natural world. By embracing technology, artists can push the boundaries of their work and create immersive experiences that challenge our understanding of the environment.

The advent of digital technology has allowed environmental artists to create works that are more dynamic and interactive. Virtual reality (VR) and augmented reality (AR) technologies, for example, enable artists to create immersive environments that transport viewers into different landscapes and ecosystems. The artist Tamiko Thiel uses VR to create interactive installations that explore themes of environmental conservation and sustainability. Her work, "Land of Cloud," allows viewers to navigate through a virtual world that changes based on their interactions, highlighting the impact of human activities on the environment.

Digital tools also allow artists to manipulate natural elements in ways that were previously impossible. For example, the artist John Gerrard uses computer modeling and simulation to create virtual landscapes that respond to real-time environmental data. His work, "Solar Reserve (Tonopah, Nevada)," is a digital simulation of a solar power plant that tracks the movement of the sun and changes in light and shadow throughout the day. By combining art and technology, Gerrard creates a powerful commentary on renewable energy and the potential of technology to address environmental challenges.

The use of technology in environmental art also allows for greater collaboration and community engagement. Online platforms and social media enable artists to share their work with a global audience and collaborate with other artists, scientists, and activists. The artist Mel Chin's project, "Fundred Dollar Bill Project," invites people from around the world to create and contribute their own hand-drawn currency notes to raise awareness about lead contamination in the environment. By harnessing the power of technology, Chin's project has engaged thousands of participants and brought attention to a critical environmental issue.

In conclusion, technology has transformed the way we create and experience environmental art. Digital tools and techniques have opened up new possibilities for artists to explore and engage with the natural world in innovative ways. By embracing technology, environmental artists can create dynamic and immersive experiences that challenge our understanding of the environment and inspire action. This chapter highlights the importance of technology in shaping the future of environmental art and its potential to drive positive change.

8

Chapter 8: The Impact of Environmental Art on Society

Environmental art has the power to influence society and drive change. Through their work, artists can raise awareness about environmental issues and inspire people to take action. Environmental art can serve as a catalyst for social and political change, encouraging people to think critically about their relationship with the environment. This chapter explores the impact of environmental art on society, highlighting how artists use their work to advocate for environmental protection and sustainability. By understanding the societal impact of environmental art, we can better appreciate its role in shaping our collective consciousness.

One of the most significant impacts of environmental art is its ability to raise awareness about environmental issues. Artists like Chris Jordan and Vik Muniz use their work to highlight the consequences of consumerism, pollution, and habitat destruction. Jordan's series, "Midway: Message from the Gyre," features haunting photographs of albatrosses that have died from ingesting plastic debris. Muniz's project, "Waste Land," involves creating large-scale portraits of waste pickers using materials collected from a landfill. By bringing attention to these issues, environmental artists can inspire viewers to reflect on their own behavior and consider ways to reduce their environmental footprint.

Environmental art can also inspire action by engaging communities and promoting collaboration. The artist Eve Mosher's project, "HighWaterLine," involved marking the projected flood zones in New York City with a blue chalk line to raise awareness about the impacts of climate change. The project engaged local communities, encouraging residents to participate in discussions about climate resilience and adaptation. Similarly, the artist JR's "Inside Out Project" invites people from around the world to contribute their own portraits to create large-scale public art installations that highlight social and environmental issues. By involving communities in the creation of art, these projects foster a sense of collective responsibility and empowerment.

The impact of environmental art extends beyond raising awareness and inspiring action; it can also influence policy and decision-making. Artists like Maya Lin and Mel Chin have used their work to advocate for environmental protection and restoration. Lin's project, "Confluence Project," involved creating a series of installations along the Columbia River to commemorate the Lewis and Clark expedition and raise awareness about the river's ecological significance. The project has helped to promote conservation efforts and engage local communities in environmental stewardship. Chin's "Operation Paydirt" project, which aims to address lead contamination in New Orleans, has brought attention to the issue and influenced policy discussions about environmental health and justice.

In conclusion, environmental art has a profound impact on society, raising awareness about critical environmental issues and inspiring individuals and communities to take action. Through their creative endeavors, environmental artists can influence public opinion, foster community engagement, and even shape policy decisions. By understanding the societal impact of environmental art, we can better appreciate its role in shaping our collective consciousness and promoting environmental stewardship.

9

Chapter 9: The Healing Power of Art

Art has the ability to heal and transform. Environmental art, in particular, can provide a sense of solace and connection to the natural world. Many artists use their work as a form of therapy, expressing their emotions and finding comfort in the creative process. This chapter delves into the therapeutic aspects of environmental art and how it can help individuals cope with stress, anxiety, and trauma. By exploring the healing power of art, we can gain a deeper understanding of its role in promoting mental and emotional well-being.

The therapeutic potential of art has been recognized for centuries. Art therapy, as a formal practice, emerged in the mid-20th century and has since gained widespread acceptance as a valuable tool for promoting mental health. Environmental art, with its focus on nature and the environment, offers unique therapeutic benefits. Engaging with nature through art can help individuals reconnect with the natural world, reducing stress and promoting a sense of calm and tranquility.

One example of the healing power of environmental art is the work of the artist Ana Mendieta. Her "Earth Body" series involved creating ephemeral sculptures using natural materials like leaves, flowers, and soil. Mendieta's art was a way for her to reconnect with her Cuban heritage and find solace in the natural world. Her work invites viewers to reflect on their own relationship with nature and find healing through that connection.

Environmental art can also provide a sense of empowerment and agency for individuals dealing with trauma and loss. The artist Andy Goldsworthy, for instance, often creates temporary sculptures using natural materials that are subject to the forces of nature. His art is a meditation on the passage of time and the impermanence of life, encouraging viewers to embrace change and find resilience in the face of adversity.

Community-based environmental art projects can also have profound therapeutic benefits. Collaborative art projects that involve creating public installations or community gardens can foster a sense of belonging and connection among participants. These projects provide opportunities for individuals to express themselves creatively, work together toward a common goal, and find support within their community.

In conclusion, the healing power of environmental art lies in its ability to reconnect individuals with the natural world and promote mental and emotional well-being. By engaging with nature through art, individuals can find solace, empowerment, and a sense of connection. This chapter highlights the therapeutic aspects of environmental art and its potential to transform lives and promote healing.

10

Chapter 10: The Future of Environmental Art

The future of environmental art is exciting and full of possibilities. As we continue to face unprecedented environmental challenges, the role of art in raising awareness and inspiring action will become increasingly important. This chapter explores the emerging trends and innovations in environmental art, highlighting the work of contemporary artists who are pushing the boundaries of this art form. By looking to the future, we can gain insight into how environmental art will continue to evolve and shape our understanding of the natural world.

One of the most promising trends in environmental art is the use of renewable and sustainable materials. Artists are increasingly exploring ways to minimize their environmental impact by using eco-friendly materials and practices. For example, the artist John Grade creates large-scale sculptures using biodegradable materials like paper and wood. His work, "Middle Fork," is a life-size replica of a hemlock tree made from reclaimed cedar, which will eventually decompose and return to the earth. By using sustainable materials, artists can create works that are both beautiful and environmentally responsible.

Another emerging trend is the use of technology to create immersive and interactive environmental art. Digital tools like virtual reality, augmented reality, and projection mapping allow artists to create dynamic and engaging experiences that can transport viewers into different landscapes and ecosystems. The artist Jenny Holzer, for example, uses projection mapping to display text and images on natural and urban surfaces, creating powerful visual narratives that highlight environmental issues. These technological innovations enable artists to reach a wider audience and create more impactful works.

Collaborative and community-based environmental art projects are also gaining momentum. Artists are increasingly working with scientists, activists, and local communities to create projects that address specific environmental challenges. For example, the artist Eve Mosher's project, "HighWaterLine," involved marking the projected flood zones in New York City with a blue chalk line to raise awareness about the impacts of climate change. By involving local communities in the creation of art, these projects foster a sense of collective responsibility and empowerment.

In conclusion, the future of environmental art is bright and full of potential. As artists continue to innovate and push the boundaries of this art form, they will play a crucial role in raising awareness about environmental issues and inspiring action. By embracing sustainable materials, technology, and community collaboration, environmental artists can create works that are both impactful and meaningful. This chapter highlights the emerging trends and innovations in environmental art and their potential to shape our understanding of the natural world.

11

Chapter 11: Personal Stories and Anecdotes

This chapter features personal stories and anecdotes from environmental artists, offering a glimpse into their creative process and the inspirations behind their work. Through these stories, we can gain a deeper appreciation of the emotional and psychological connections that drive environmental art. By sharing their experiences, artists can inspire others to explore their own creative potential and find new ways to connect with the environment.

One such story is that of the artist Patrick Dougherty, known for his whimsical "stickwork" sculptures. Dougherty began working with natural materials after realizing the immense creative potential of sticks and branches. His sculptures, often resembling nests or huts, evoke a sense of playfulness and wonder. Dougherty's work is inspired by his childhood spent exploring the woods and building forts, and he aims to recreate that sense of adventure and imagination in his art.

Another inspiring story comes from the artist Agnes Denes, whose project "Wheatfield – A Confrontation" involved planting a two-acre wheat field in downtown Manhattan. The project, created in 1982, drew attention to the stark contrast between urban development and agricultural land, sparking conversations about sustainability and food security. Denes' work is a testament to the power of environmental art to raise awareness about critical issues and inspire change.

The artist Chris Jordan's journey into environmental art began with his fascination with data and statistics. Jordan's series, "Running the Numbers," uses large-scale photographs to illustrate the staggering scale of consumer waste and its environmental impact. His work aims to make abstract data more tangible and relatable, encouraging viewers to reflect on their own consumption habits and consider ways to reduce waste.

These personal stories and anecdotes highlight the diverse inspirations and motivations behind environmental art. By sharing their experiences, artists can inspire others to explore their own creative potential and find new ways to connect with the environment. This chapter offers a glimpse into the emotional and psychological connections that drive environmental art, enriching our understanding and appreciation of this unique art form.

12

Chapter 12: Conclusion

Environmental art is a powerful and transformative art form that challenges us to see the world through different lenses. By exploring the psychological roots of environmental art, we can gain a deeper understanding of our own relationship with the natural world. This book has provided an overview of the key concepts and themes in environmental art, highlighting the intricate connections between mindscapes and landscapes. As we move forward, it is important to continue exploring and appreciating the beauty and complexity of environmental art, recognizing its role in shaping our understanding of the environment and our place within it.

Environmental art has the power to raise awareness about critical environmental issues, inspire action, and promote healing and connection. By embracing the diversity of cultural perspectives, integrating scientific knowledge, and leveraging technological innovations, environmental artists can create works that are both impactful and meaningful. This book has highlighted the importance of environmental art in shaping our collective consciousness and promoting environmental stewardship.

In conclusion, environmental art is a profound and transformative art form that captures the essence of our connection with nature. By exploring the psychological roots of environmental art, we can gain a deeper understanding of our own relationship with the natural world and be inspired to take action to protect it. As we move forward, let us continue to appreciate and support the work of environmental artists, recognizing their vital role in shaping a more sustainable and harmonious future.

Book Description for "Mindscapes and Landscapes: Exploring the Psychological Roots of Environmental Art"

In "Mindscapes and Landscapes: Exploring the Psychological Roots of Environmental Art," we embark on a captivating journey that unveils the profound connections between the human psyche and the natural world. This thought-provoking book delves into the essence of environmental art, tracing its roots from ancient cave paintings to contemporary masterpieces. It examines how artists across cultures and eras have used their work to reflect, challenge, and inspire our understanding of nature.

Through twelve engaging chapters, the book explores the intricate relationship between art, psychology, and the environment. Readers will discover how environmental art taps into our subconscious, evokes powerful emotions, and fosters a deep appreciation for the beauty and fragility of the natural world. The book highlights the impact of cultural influences, scientific knowledge, and technological innovations on environmental art, showcasing the diverse ways in which artists express their connection to nature.

Featuring personal stories and anecdotes from renowned environmental artists, "Mindscapes and Landscapes" offers a glimpse into their creative processes and the inspirations behind their work. The book also explores the therapeutic potential of environmental art, revealing how it can promote mental and emotional well-being.

As we face unprecedented environmental challenges, this book emphasizes the vital role of environmental art in raising awareness, inspiring action, and shaping a more sustainable future. "Mindscapes and Landscapes" is a must-read for anyone passionate about art, nature, and the profound connections that bind them. Join us on this enlightening journey and discover the transformative power of environmental art.